MW00652461

OLSAT®
PRACTICE TEST

Grade 5 (6th Grade Entry) & Grade 4 (5th Grade Entry)
LEVEL E

Test 2

Written and Edited by:
Gifted and Talented OLSAT Test Prep Team

ISBN: 978-0997768077

Origins Publications
New York, NY, USA

Email:info@originspublications

ABOUT ORIGINS PUBLICATIONS

Origins Publications and the OLSAT® Test Prep Team helps students develop their higher-order thinking skills while also improving their chances of admission into gifted and accelerated learner programs.

Our goal is to unleash and nurture the genius in every student. We do this by offering educational and test prep materials that are fun, challenging and provide a sense of accomplishment.

Please contact us with any questions.

info@originspublications.com

Contents

Origins Publications ©

PREPARATION GUIDE

Part 1. Introduction to the OLSAT-E

The Otis Lennon School Ability Test (OLSAT) is an important exam; the more you know about it, the better you will fare. This guide offers an overview of the types of questions that are likely to be on the test, some test-taking strategies to improve performance during preparation and on test day, and sample OLSAT© tests that students can use to test their knowledge and practice their test-taking skills.

Why the OLSAT-E?

Many gifted and talented programs and highly-selective public schools across the USA require students to pass an exam in order to be admitted to the school or program. The OLSAT-E is often used as an assessment tool or admissions test in 4th and 5th grade for entry into 5th and 6th grade of highly-competitive programs and schools.

Who Takes The OLSAT-E?

Fourth and fifth graders who want to gain admission to fifth and sixth grade in a gifted and talented program, or highly-selective school. The OLSAT-E can also be used as an assessment tool by teachers to decipher which students would benefit from an accelerated or remedial curriculum.

When Does the OLSAT Take Place?

This depends on the school district you reside in, or want to attend. Check with the relevant school/district to learn more about test dates and the application/registration process.

OLSAT© Level E Overview

The OLSAT® is a test of abstract thinking and an individual's ability to reason logically. It measures verbal, quantitative, and spatial reasoning ability. In taking the OLSAT®, students will be evaluated on their ability to perceive information accurately, understand relationships and patterns among objects, reason through abstract problems, apply generalizations, and recall and evaluate information.

The OLSAT® covers topics that students may not see in school, so kids will need to think a little differently in order to do well. A student's stress management and time management skills are also tested during the nearly hour-long exam.

Length

The OLSAT® Level E test is a 40-minute test.

Format

The entire test is made up of 72 multiple choice questions. The questions are distributed as follows:

VERBAL		NONVERBAL	
Verbal Comprehension		**Figural Reasoning**	
Antonyms	4	Figural Analogies	6
Sentence Arrangement	4	Figural Series	6
Sentence Completion	4	Pattern Matrices	6
Verbal Reasoning		**Quantitative Reasoning**	
Arithmetic Reasoning	4	Number Inferences	6
Logical Selection	4	Pattern Matrices	6
Inferences	4	Number Series	6
Verbal Analogies	4		
Verbal Classification	4		
Word/letter matrices	4	**TOTAL QUESTIONS**	72

Test Sections

The test consists of verbal material and nonverbal material. The verbal material consists of verbal comprehension and verbal reasoning questions, while the nonverbal material consists of figural reasoning and quantitative reasoning questions.

Verbal Material

VERBAL COMPREHENSION QUESTIONS

The verbal comprehension questions are aimed at measuring students' ability to gather and manipulate information from language. In particular, these questions seek to evaluate how students understand the way words and sentences relate to each other, and also how students interpret nuances in language.

There are three types of verbal comprehension questions:

✓ **Antonyms:** These questions require students to search for the opposite meaning of a given word within the answer choices provided. In particular, this group of questions aims to evaluate a student's vocabulary skills. Ultimately, these questions require a sophisticated understanding of vocabulary because students have to not only comprehend a word, but also understand it enough so that they can recognize its true opposite.

✓ **Sentence Arrangement**: These questions provide students with sentences that have been mixed up. Looking at this jumbled set of words, students must piece the words together to compose a complete thought. These questions assess a student's ability to understand the structure of language by asking them to take fragmented parts and, from them, create a whole.

✓ **Sentence Completion**: With these questions students will have to "fill in the blank(s)." The answer options outline a number of words that could be used to complete a given sentence. However, students must choose the words that create a complete, logical sentence.

VERBAL REASONING QUESTIONS

The verbal reasoning component of the test measures a student's ability to comprehend patterns, relationships, and context clues in writing in order to solve a problem. In order to be successful in answering these questions, students must be able to fully understand what a question is asking, as well as make inferences based on what they have read.

The verbal reasoning questions on the test are composed of six different question types:

✓ **Arithmetic Reasoning**: These verbal problems incorporate mathematical reasoning. Some questions assess basic concepts, including counting, and estimation. Others assess more sophisticated concepts such as reasoning and solving word problems. The main skill tested here is the ability to create mathematical problems from language and to solve those problems.

✓ **Inferences**: Students will be provided an argument or scenario and, based on the information provided, must discern an appropriate conclusion. These questions rely on a student's ability to evaluate which parts of the provided information are absolutely necessary for reaching the correct conclusion.

✓ **Logical Selection**: In order to find the answers to these questions, students have to apply logical reasoning to uncover the best answer. These questions often asks students to consider which answer *might* be correct, versus which answer options are *always* correct. Being able to make that distinction is key.

✓ **Verbal Analogies:** These questions ask students to consider the relationship between a pair of words, then apply this relationship to another pair of words. Students' ability to correctly uncover these relationships is key to answering these type of questions.

✓ **Verbal Classification**: With these questions, students must look at a series of words or concepts and identify which one does not fit with the others. In answering this type of question, students must be able to evaluate the relationships among words.

✓ **Word/letter matrices**: These questions provide students with a matrix of letters or words. Students must perceive the pattern or relationship among these words in order to supply a missing letter or word.

Non-Verbal Material
FIGURAL REASONING QUESTIONS

The purpose of these questions is to measure a student's ability to reason their way through non-language based scenarios. These questions take a more visual format than the verbal questions, incorporating geometric figures instead of words. Students will be expected to find the relationship between numbers or objects in a pattern, to predict and create what the next level of the pattern will look like, and generalize the rules they discover.

There are four figural reasoning question types:

✓ **Figural Analogies**: Like verbal analogies, these questions require students to identify the relationship of a given pair. With these questions, however, students are asked to examine the relationship between figures instead of words. Once students have uncovered this relationship, they then must apply this rule to a second pair of figures. This question type assesses the student's ability to infer a relationship between a pair of geometric shapes and select the shape that is related to the stimulus in the same way.

✓ **Figural Classification**: In these questions, students must examine a group of figures and identify a pattern or principle that links those figures. Then, students must conclude which of the answer choices follows this same principle.

✓ **Figural Series**: With this series of questions, students must look at a series of geometric figures, discern a pattern within the series, and find the 'missing' drawing/shape in the pattern.

✓ **Pattern Matrices**: This question asks the student to supply a missing element in a matrix of geometric shapes. These questions test a student's ability to discern rules in a pattern and evaluate how those rules govern a series of geometric figures.

QUANTITATIVE REASONING QUESTIONS

These questions evaluates a student's ability to discern patterns and relationships in order to solve problems with numbers. This section requires that students be able to predict outcomes based on their knowledge of mathematics.

There are three types of quantitative reasoning questions:

✓ **Numeric Inferences**: Using computation skills, students will have to determine how two or three numbers are related. Once they have uncovered this relationship, students will have to apply this rule to another pair or trio of numbers.

✓ **Number Matrices**: For these questions, students must examine numbers in a matrix and determine what principle or rule links those numbers. Then, they must apply this rule to figure out what number should be placed in a given blank.

✓ **Number Series**: Students must examine a sequence of numbers and determine a pattern that governs those numbers. They will then apply that pattern in order to predict what comes next.

Part 2. Using This Book

You have made an important first step towards ensuring your child will do her best on test day by purchasing this book. This Preparation Guide offers general strategies your child can use to tackle the test. Your child can also prepare for the exam by taking the practice test in this book.

Performance on the practice test can help identify a stu-dent's weaknesses and allow your child to focus on questions that most need to be reviewed.

When to Start Studying?

Every family and student will approach preparation for this test differently. There is no 'right' way to prepare; there is only the best way for a particular child and family. Some take the 'cram' approach, loading up on as many hours as possible before the test date. Other parents think too much focus on preparation may create anxiety in their child that could backfire on test day. In this case, a more low-key approach may work best.

With that said, repeated exposure to the format and nature of the test will help a student prepare for this challenging test. We suggest students, at minimum, take one practice test (preferably under timed conditions) and spend a minimum of 8-10 hours working through OLSAT® type questions.

As they say, knowledge is power! And preparing for the OLSAT also gives students a chance to know what they are up against. This alone can help a fifth-grader not panic on test day when faced with unfamiliar and perplexing questions. The OLSAT measures a student's academic performance but also his ability to manage time efficiently and capacity to keep his wits under pressure.

Part 3: Exam Preparation and Test-Taking Strategies

Preparing for the OLSAT in many ways follows the same process as preparing for any other exam—your child needs to review the concepts he or she already knows and boost skills in areas that he or she is unfamiliar with. You can diagnose your child's weaknesses by analyzing her scores on the practice test in this book. Then, focus study time on reviewing and practicing more of the question types that your child finds tricky or regularly stumbles on.

General Test Taking Strategies For OLSAT® Level E Test

The OLSAT® Level E does not just test your child's knowledge and skills in specific verbal and non-verbal areas, but also her test-taking skills. If your child knows the material on which she will be tested and is familiar with test-taking techniques and strategies, it will certainly improve her chances of doing well on the exam.

Help your child prepare for the test by using the following tips and strategies.

✓ KNOW THE TEST

The content and required pacing on this test is very challenging for a fifth grader. A student will need to sustain focus throughout the test. Because of this, it is important that your child is familiar with the format, nature and structure of the exam, and that he or she works on sample questions and takes practice tests in timed conditions.

As a general test preparation strategy, we recommend that you first review each question type with your child and ask him or her to solve practice questions without a time restriction. Then, spend time analysing the answers and explanations (both incorrect and correct) for each question.

In order to succeed on the test, a student must keep calm and learn to use time wisely. That's why we recommend that students take several timed practice tests, which helps build stamina and confidence, as well as ensures that a student does not waste time on test day panicking about the unknown! A practice test also helps a student get used to reading each question carefully but quickly, and figure out the best and fastest way to transfer answers and mark the bubbles in the answer sheet. For example, practicing the simple technique of shading the bubbles quickly and efficiently can help a student gain a minute or two during the test.

Use the scores on the practice tests to identify subject areas or question types where your child is struggling. If you have limited time to prepare, spend most energy reviewing areas where your child is encountering the majority of problems.

✓ DON'T LET DIFFICULT QUESTIONS UNDERMINE CONFIDENCE

Be prepared for difficult questions on the test from the get go! The OLSAT® is not given in an 'adaptive' format -- where each subsequent question increases in difficulty. The make-up of the exam is as follows; about half of the OLSAT® Level E is made up of "easy" questions, the answers to which most fifth graders will know. More than a third of the questions will be of medium difficulty, and students who receive close to a 'mean' score will also answer these correctly. In general, a student's strategy should be to avoid thoughtless mistakes and to solve these questions relatively quickly. About 18% of questions are difficult for most students. The students who answer some or all of these questions correctly are the ones that have the highest chance of being admitted to the assessing program or school.

So what to do when stumped with a tough question? First, a student needs to stay calm and focused. She can spend some extra time (but not too much!) on the challenging question (knowing that there are easier questions ahead which can be answered faster). If she is still unable to figure out the answer, she should make an educated guess and move on to the next question.

✓ USE PROCESS OF ELIMINATION

If a student is stumped by a question, she can use the process of elimination. Firstly, eliminate obviously wrong answers in order to narrow down the answer choices. If still in doubt after using this technique, she can make an educated guess. Process of elimination is a key technique that helps improve the probability of selecting the correct response even if a student is not sure about how to answer a question.

✓ NEVER LEAVE AN ANSWER BLANK

On the OLSAT® test, no points are deducted for wrong answers. Therefore, when all else fails, educated guessing should be used as a strategy. When a student finishes the test and has time to spare, he should review the answer sheet to ensure EVERY question has a marked answer.

✓ MARK UP THE TEST

Mark up the booklet as much as you need to as you take the test. If you find something that looks important, underline it, make notes in the margins, circle facts, cross out answers that are wrong, and draw diagrams.

✓ USE TIME WISELY

The OLSAT® Level E asks students to answer 72 questions in 40 minutes. This means a student has just over 30 seconds to answer each question. On test day, a student should always be aware of the time. Scanning ahead and seeing how many questions remain in the test will help him or her gauge how much time to allocate for each question.

✓ DEVELOP FIGURAL REASONING SKILLS

On the nonverbal material, the object is to use clues to find specific patterns and relationships, and then to apply that relationship or pattern to the answer options to identify the correct one among five choices. This includes finding similarities and differences between items or sets of geometric figures, predicting the next step in a progression of geometric shapes, or supplying a missing element in a matrix. In order to improve at this aspect of the test, we suggest students spend time doing activities such as puzzles, Sudoku, chess and/or Rubik's cube, all of which help develop a child's ability to identify and interpret patterns.

✓ IMPROVE VOCABULARY & READING COMPREHENSION

The verbal material on the test is the most difficult to prep for as it requires a child to have a large vocabulary and excellent reading comprehension. This is built up over time by reading widely and analysing what is read. If your child is preparing well enough in advance, he can spend time on building vocabulary using flashcards or, even better, learning and reviewing roots, prefixes and suffixes of words. A student can use the other general test-taking strategies to improve his score on the verbal section even if his vocabulary is not strong. However, strengthening vocabulary is a potential way to do better on the test.

✓ IGNORE ALL DISTRACTIONS

You may have tried to re-create the exact test-taking atmosphere during practice exams. But when your child goes for the real thing she will be in a room with many other kids, maybe even someone with a cold who is sneezing or coughing. Tell her to ignore it all and concentrate on her test.

✓ MANAGE TEST DAY JITTERS

Avoid squeezing in a last-minute review. Instead, encourage your child to visualize his success and plan a reward for after the test is over. Encourage your child to think positive when there's a frustrating question. Freezing up and thinking all kinds of negative ideas will only kill confidence during the exam. Instead, teach your child to use positive self-talk, including "I've studied this," "I can do this," and "I can figure this problem out." If your child finds himself getting anxious, tell him to help himself relax by taking long, deep breaths.

• KEEP THINGS IN PERSPECTIVE

Yes, the OLSAT-E is an important exam, but it needs to be put in context. Tell your child that even if he does poorly on the exam, it is not the end of the world. His family won't stop loving him. He won't be less of a person. Perspective is important to perfor-mance. Of course your child should be serious about succeeding on the test. But he should not lose sight of other important aspects of life.

Strategies for the Final Days before the Exam

The weeks or months of preparation will soon pay off. You have worked hard, and the test is just a week away. Here are some tips for making sure things go smoothly in the home stretch.

The Week before the Test:

- Be sure you know exactly where you are taking the test. Get detailed directions. Take a practice transit trip so you know exactly how long it will take to get there.
- Review everything you have learned.
- Get quality sleep each night.
- Practice visualization - see yourself performing well on the test.

The Day before the Test:

- Get to bed early.
- Get light exercise.
- Get everything you will need ready: pencils/pens, a watch, admission materials/documentation, and water or any mints or snacks you would like to have along.
- Make a list of everything you need to bring so you don't forget anything in the morning.

The Day of the Test:

- Eat a light, healthy breakfast, such as yogurt and granola or a low-fat, low-sugar cereal and fruit.
- Dress comfortably. Wear layers so that you can take off a sweatshirt or sweater if you are too warm in the test room.
- Avoid squeezing in a last-minute review. Instead, visualize your success and plan your reward for after the test is over.
- Think positive!

What to Bring to the Test

- ✓ A watch
- ✓ Water
- ✓ Two number 2 pencils with erasers and two black or blue ink pens
- ✓ Sweatshirt or sweater

In a manila envelope, also bring the following to complete the admissions process:

- ✓ Copies of your child's most recent report card
- ✓ Copies of the 4th grade NYS Exam in ELA/ Math or ERB
- ✓ Copy of your child's end of the year 4th grade report card
- ✓ Self-addressed stamped envelope

OLSAT© Level E Practice Test 2

1.

The opposite of **novice** is:

A. beginner   **B.** know-it-all   **C.** intermediate   **D.** professional   **E.** expert

2.

The drawings in the box go together in a certain way. Which drawing goes where you see the question mark?

          A   B   C   D   E

3.

Page is to **book** as **brick** is to:

A. building   **B.** concrete   **C.** hard   **D.** heavy   **E.** fire

4.

The drawings below form a series. Which drawing completes that series and goes where you see the question mark?

          A   B   C   D   E

5.

Homes always have:

A. two stories   **B.** several rooms   **C.** beds   **D.** inhabitants   **E.** pets

6.

You probably _____ the test because you didn't _____ the material.

A. passed — study

B. failed — read

C. wrote — like

D. questioned — forgot

E. aced — understand

7.

Which word does **not** go with the others?

A. shine   **B.** shackles   **C.** shirts   **D.** shades   **E.** shakes

8.

Liza is older than Madison, but younger than Tiffany. We know for certain that:

A. Tiffany is the most mature.

B. The three are sisters.

C. Tiffany is the eldest.

D. Liza and Madison are two years apart.

E. Tiffany is older by at least three years.

9.

 is to as is to:

                                                   A   B   C   D   E

10.

If the words were arranged to make the **best** sentence, with which letter would the **second** word of the sentence begin?

mine	hand	your	put	in

A. p   **B.** y   **C.** h   **D.** i   **E.** m

11.

Note is to **scale** as:

A. Star is to constellation.

B. Book is to chapter.

C. Singer is to album.

D. Ink is to paper.

E. Recipe is to meal.

Origins Publications ©

12.

The words in the box go together in a certain way. Which word goes where you see the question mark?

on	son	song
an	?	mane

A. ant   **B.** san   **C.** man   **D.** ton   **E.** ban

13.

The drawings below form a series. Which drawing continues that series and goes where you see the question mark?

A   B   C   D   E

14.

Be sure to _____ the dishes that were _____ during the dinner.

A. wash — dirtied

B. clean — broken

C. find — used

D. dirty — cleaned

E. wipe — scratched

15.

 is to as is to:

A   B   C   D   E

16.

Grass is to **plain** as:

A. Water is to ocean.

B. Sand is to beach.

C. Polar bear is to glacier.

D. Root is to tree.

E. Stem is to flower.

17.

The numbers in each box go together following the same rule. Figure out that rule and then apply it to the third box. What number goes where you see the question mark?

| 1, 2, 8 | 2, 4, 16 | 3, 6, ? |

A. 24   **B.** 18   **C.** 20   **D.** 12   **E.** 8

18.

A meal cannot be eaten without:

A. friends   **B.** food   **C.** a cafeteria   **D.** forks   **E.** a beverage

19.

If the words were arranged to make the **best** sentence, with which letter would the **second** word of the sentence begin?

| found | Sarah | never | toy's | batteries | the |

A. s   **B.** n   **C.** f   **D.** t   **E.** b

20.

The drawings in the box go together in a certain way. Which drawing goes where you see the question mark?

A   B   C   D   E

21.

The numbers in each box go together following the same rule. Figure out that rule and then apply it to the third box. What number goes where you see the question mark?

| 2, 8 | 3, 12 | ?, 20 |

A. 8   **B.** 6   **C.** 5   **D.** 4   **E.** 10

22.

What comes next in the series?   A   11   C   13   E   15   G   17   ?

A. J   **B.** 19   **C.** H   **D.** I   **E.** 18

23.

The numbers in each box go together following the same rule.Figure out that rule and then apply it to the third box. What number goes where you see the question mark?

| 9, 12, 15 | 7, 10, 13 | 5, ?,11 |

A. 7 **B.** 8 **C.** 10 **D.** 12 **E.** 9

24.

The words in the box go together in a certain way. Which word goes where you see the question mark?

| cart | catastrophe | caramel |
| shirt | shame | ? |

A. same **B.** carousel **C.** shallow **D.** savior **E.** silhouette

25.

The opposite of **clean** is:

A. old **B.** new **C.** spotless **D.** dirty **E.** rusted

26.

Todd won more prizes at the arcade than Matthew, but fewer than Spencer. If Todd won eight prizes, two of which were toys and four of which were candy, we know for certain that:

A. Spencer spent the most money at the arcade.

B. Mathew likes toys more than candy.

C. Spencer won at least three toys.

D. Matthew didn't win any prizes.

E. Spencer won at least nine prizes total.

27.

Stacy has thirty-four papers in a pile.Some of the papers are red, some a green, and some are blue.Stacy has ten red papers. If she has three times as many green papers as blue papers, how many green papers does she have?

A. 12 **B.** 9 **C.** 30 **D.** 8 **E.** 18

28.

The numbers in the box go together in a certain way. Which number goes where you see the question mark?

3	14	18
4	21	?
5	28	36

A. 30   **B.** 3   **C.** 29   **D.** 24   **E.** 27

29.

If the words were arranged to make the **best** sentence, with which letter would the **third** word of the sentence begin?

class	we	in	met	science

A. w   **B.** m   **C.** i   **D.** s   **E.** c

30.

We were all surprised that she wore such a(n) _____ dress to the dance because she usually dressed plainly.

A. unique   **B.** severe   **C.** simple   **D.** fancy   **E.** feminine

31.

Which word does **not** go with the others?

A. oak   **B.** pine   **C.** acorn   **D.** maple   **E.** willow

32.

What number is missing in this series?   29   13   27   13   ?   13   23   13   21

A. 15   **B.** 11   **C.** 25   **D.** 24   **E.** 26

33.

The drawings in the box go together in a certain way. Which drawing goes where you see the question mark?

A   B   C   D   E

Origins Publications ©

34.

The numbers in the box go together in a certain way. Which number goes where you see the question mark?

5,6	1,7	6,1,5,7
2,3	?	3,4,2,9

A. 9,4   **B.** 2,9   **C.** 4,3   **D.** 4,9   **E.** 3,4

35.

 is to as � is to:

```
     ▷ |        |   |        ▶ |        | ◁      | ▼ |
                | △ |                            |   |
      A            B            C            D        E
```

36.

What number is five less than three times seven?

A. 8   **B.** 33   **C.** 16   **D.** 26   **E.** 11

37.

Coffee is to **beverage** as **pie** is to:

A. meal   **B.** dinner   **C.** snack   **D.** dessert   **E.** blueberry

38.

What goes where you see the question mark in this series?   E   7   2   G   12   5   I   19   10   K   ?   16

A. M   **B.** 27   **C.** 23   **D.** 28   **E.** 25

39.

The numbers in the box go together in a certain way. Which number goes where you see the question mark?

5	18	31
11	24	?

A. 32   **B.** 29   **C.** 35   **D.** 40   **E.** 37

40.

The words in the box go together in a certain way. Which word goes where you see the question mark?

eat	beat	seat
ate	?	sate

A. bate   **B.** bare   **C.** feat   **D.** fate   **E.** arts

41.

The drawings in the box go together in a certain way. Which drawing goes where you see the question mark?

                    A   **B**   **C**   **D**   **E**

42.

Last school week, Mrs. Smith, Mr. Carter, and Ms. Davis all assigned homework. Mrs. Smith assigned homework each day except Thursday. If Mr. Carter assigned less homework than Mrs. Smith but more than Ms. Davis, then we know for certain that:

A. Ms. Davis didn't assign any homework.

B. Mr. Carter didn't assign homework on Thursday.

C. Mr. Carter assigned homework a maximum of three days.

D. Ms. Davis assigned homework two days.

E. Mr. Carter assigned homework two days.

43.

What number comes next in this series?   7   18   14   25   21   32   ?

A. 30   **B.** 18   **C.** 24   **D.** 22   **E.** 28

44.

 is to as is to:

A   **B**   **C**   **D**   **E**

45.

The opposite of **hot** is:

A. fire   **B.** cold   **C.** cool   **D.** snow   **E.** warm

46.

Madison has sixty books on her bookshelf. Some of the books are fiction books and the others are nonfiction. If she has four times as many fiction books as nonfiction books, how may fiction books does she have?

A. 20   **B.** 40   **C.** 48   **D.** 12   **E.** 24

47.

If the words were arranged to make the **best** sentence, with which letter would the **first** word of the sentence begin?

| at | house | party | Timothy's | the | will | be |

A. t   **B.** h   **C.** p   **D.** w   **E.** b

48.

The drawings in the box go together in a certain way. Which drawing goes where you see the question mark?

A   B   C   D   E

49.

A book cannot be read without:

A. a teacher   **B.** a story   **C.** people   **D.** words   **E.** pictures

50.

The drawings below form a series. Which drawing continues that series and goes where you see the question mark?

A   B   C   D   E

51.

The numbers in the box go together in a certain way. Which number goes where you see the question mark?

| 9 | 12 | 15 |
| 11 | 14 | ? |

A. 17 **B.** 16 **C.** 18 **D.** 19 **E.** 13

52.

The drawings below form a series. Which drawing continues that series and goes where you see the question mark?

A   B   C   D   E

53.

After Lori fired some of her employees, she had to _____ work on the project until she could hire more people.

A. inspire **B.** postpone **C.** gift **D.** start **E.** alternate

54.

 is to as is to:

A   B   C   D   E

55.

Larry has several different apps on his phone.Each of the apps is one of three types: some of the apps are games, while others are educational, and some are for reading the news. If Larry has a total of twelve apps and three of them are games, we know for certain that:

A. Larry likes to read the news more than use games.

B. Larry doesn't use games very often.

C. He does not have the same number of educational and news apps

D. Larry spent a lot of money on apps for his phone.

E. Larry has a total of four news apps.

Origins Publications ©

56.

The numbers in each box go together following the same rule. Figure out that rule and then apply it to the third box. What number goes where you see the question mark?

2, 14   3, 21   4, ?

A. 24   **B.** 28   **C.** 26   **D.** 30   **E.** 32

57.

The words in the box go together in a certain way. Which word goes where you see the question mark?

sag	slug	stung
bat	belt	?

A. swift   **B.** ban   **C.** bolt   **D.** blurt   **E.** start

58.

A piano cannot be played without:

A. a song   **B.** fingers   **C.** a conductor   **D.** singing   **E.** music sheets

59.

The numbers in the box go together in a certain way. Which numbers go where you see the question marks?

3	18	9
?	36	18
7	42	?

A. 6, 22   **B.** 5, 25   **C.** 4, 24   **D.** 4, 21   **E.** 6, 21

60.

 is to as is to:

A   B   C   D   E

61.

The drawings below form a series. Which drawing continues that series and goes where you see the question mark?

A   B   C   D   E

62.

Which word does **not** go with the others?

A. addition **B.** subtraction **C.** multiplication **D.** division **E.** fractions

63.

What number is four more than six times eight?

A. 52 **B.** 32 **C.** 44 **D.** 20 **E.** 54

64.

The drawings below form a series. Which drawing continues that series and goes where you see the question mark?

A B C D E

65.

Which word does **not** go with the others?

A. jump **B.** pounce **C.** leap **D.** spring **E.** skip

66.

The drawings in the box go together in a certain way. Which drawing goes where you see the question mark?

A B C D E

67.

The numbers in each box go together following the same rulE. Figure out that rule and then apply it to the third box. What number goes where you see the question mark?

2, 6 4, 9 6, ?   **A.** 8 **B.** 10 **C.** 9 **D.** 12 **E.** 13

68.

The opposite of **enter** is:

A. in   **B.** go   **C.** exit   **D.** entrance   **E.** finish

69.

The numbers in each box go together following the same rulE. Figure out that rule and then apply it to the third box. What number goes where you see the question mark?

| 12, 3 | 20, 5 | 32, ? |

A. 8   **B.** 6   **C.** 9   **D.** 4   **E.** 7

70.

The numbers in the box go together in a certain way. Which number goes where you see the question mark?

| 23 | 18 | 13 |
| 19 | 14 | ? |

A. 5   **B.** 10   **C.** 9   **D.** 8   **E.** 11

71.

 is to as is to:

     A   B   C   D   E

72.

The numbers in the box go together in a certain way. Which number goes where you see the question mark?

| 32 | 8 | 2 |
| 48 | 12 | ? |

A. 8   **B.** 2   **C.** 4   **D.** 6   **E.** 3

Answer Key Practice Test 2

Number	Correct Answer	Type of Question
1	E	antonym
2	A	pattern matrix
3	A	verbal analogy
4	C	figural series
5	D	logical selection
6	B	sentence completion
7	A	verbal classification
8	C	inference
9	C	figural analogy
10	B	sentence arrangement
11	A	verbal analogy
12	C	word matrix
13	E	figural series
14	A	sentence completion
15	C	figural analogy
16	B	verbal analogy
17	A	number series
18	B	logical selection
19	E	sentence arrangement
20	E	pattern matrix
21	C	number series
22	D	number series
23	B	number series
24	C	word matrix
25	D	antonym
26	E	inference
27	E	arithmetic reasoning
28	E	number matrix
29	C	sentence arrangement
30	D	sentence completion
31	C	verbal classification
32	C	number series
33	C	pattern matrix
34	D	number matrix
35	D	figural analogy
36	C	arithmetic reasoning

Number	Correct Answer	Type of Question
37	D	verbal analogy
38	B	number series
39	E	number matrix
40	A	word matrix
41	B	pattern matrix
42	C	inference
43	E	number series
44	C	figural analogy
45	B	antonym
46	C	arithmetic reasoning
47	A	sentence arrangement
48	E	pattern matrix
49	D	logical selection
50	E	figural series
51	A	number matrix
52	B	figural series
53	B	sentence completion
54	D	figural analogy
55	C	Inference
56	B	number series
57	D	word matrix
58	B	logical selection
59	E	number matrix
60	D	figural analogy
61	E	figural series
62	E	verbal classification
63	A	arithmetic reasoning
64	E	figural series
65	E	verbal classification
66	A	pattern matrix
67	D	number series
68	C	antonym
69	A	number series
70	C	number matrix
71	B	figural analogy
72	E	number matrix

Answers Explanations Practice Test 2

1. Correct Answer: E

This question is looking for the antonym of the word <u>novice</u>, which means a beginner. Students may be tempted to choose answer D, as someone who is the opposite of a beginner may be professional; however, this is not a true opposite. Choice E is the only answer that makes sense.

2. Correct Answer: A

As we progress from left to right, the pattern in the top row shows that the small circle in the square moves from the top-left position to the bottom-right and then to the top-right. At the same time it alternates its highlighting from dark to light and then back to dark. The same pattern applies on the second row. The square inside the circle will move from the top-left position to the bottom-right and then to the top-right. It will also alternate its highlighting. Therefore, the missing figure in the second position must be a circle, eliminating choices C and D. The small square must be positioned inside in the bottom-right position, which eliminates choice B. Only choices A and E remain. The correct choice is A, because the square must alternate its highlighting from dark to light.

3. Correct Answer: A

With this question, the key is to figure out the relationship between the words provided in the analogy. It helps to put the words in a sentence to evaluate their relationship. We might say, that "many pages make up a book." We know, then, that this analogy shows us a very small part of a much larger whole. We can also say that "many bricks make up a building," which means that choice A is the correct answer. Concrete, option B, is incorrect because bricks are not a composite, or part of, concrete. The answer options C and D describe bricks, but they do not complete the part to whole analogy. Additionally, the answer option E of "fire" doesn't exhibit a clear relationship to bricks.

4. Correct Answer: C

The first three drawings are all different from each other. The first drawing is a square, a circle, and a shaded hexagon; the second drawing is a hexagon, a shaded square, and a circle; and the third drawing is a shaded circle, a hexagon, and a square. We can also see that the fifth figure is the same as the second figure. This indicates that the group of the first three shapes starts to repeat, which means the fourth shape must also be the same as the first shape. Choice C is the same drawing as the first drawing in the series and completes the pattern of three different figures that repeat.

5. Correct Answer: D

With this question, the key is finding the answer option that is something all homes have. Students may want to choose options B or C, as these are likely things that homes often have. However, a home—like an apartment, for example—could be one room, so that would rule out answer option B. Additionally, while most homes do have a bed, it is possible that not all homes contain beds. The only answer that works is option D because, by definition, a home is a place where a person lives.

6. Correct Answer: B

In answering this question, it's important to consider both of the blanks. The words used to fill these blanks have a cause and effect relationship, so students have to be alert for this correlation. The only set of answers that works is option B. However, there are several answer options where one word will make sense. For example, it would make sense to say that someone <u>passed</u> a test or <u>aced</u> a test; however, these answer options fall apart when we fill in the second blank. It would not make sense to say that someone <u>passed</u> a test because they did not <u>study</u>, or that someone <u>aced</u> a test because they did not <u>understand</u> the material. The other answer options—C and D—have answer options that don't really make sense in either blank.

7. Correct Answer: A

With this question, we have to look for a pattern in the answer options. Most of the answers start with "sh" and ends with "s." We have: shackles, shirts, shades, and shakes. The only answer option that does not belong is <u>shine</u> because, though it starts with an "sh," it does not end with an "s." Therefore, this (choice A) is our correct answer, as this option is unlike the others.

8. Correct Answer: C

Based on the information provided in this question, we know that the order of these girls' ages, from oldest to youngest, is Tiffany, Liza, then Madison. Other than this, we don't know anything for certain; everything else besides answer option C is a guess rather than a fact.

9. Correct Answer: C

In the first pair of this figural analogy, we can see that the hexagon rotates by 180 degrees and then reverses its highlighting so that the light sections become dark and the dark sections become light. To find the missing figure, we must rotate the circle by 180 degrees and reverse its highlighting. By reversing the highlighting, the circle we are looking for will have only one of its sections unshaded. Answer A is eliminated, because it is a hexagon and not a circle. Answers B and D are also eliminated because they have more than one unshaded section. The correct answer is C because it has been rotated by exactly 180 degrees before reversing its highlighting.

10. Correct Answer: B

In order to answer this question, students must first arrange the sentence correctly. The completed sentence should read, "Put your hand in mine." Then, students must identify the first letter of the second word of the sentence: "y." The correct choice is therefore option B.

11. Correct Answer: A

We know that analogies are all about determining the relationship between words. If we make a sentence to show the relationship in this question, we might say that a "note is part of a scale." In looking at the answer options, students need to ask themselves what other pair of words would fit equally well in this sentence. Out of all the options, a "star is part of a constellation" makes the most sense. Therefore, choice A is the correct answer.

12. Correct Answer: C

The key to this question is determining the relationship between the words. In the top row, each word, moving from left to right, has an additional letter. The base word is <u>on</u>. To get the next word, we've added a letter— an s— to the beginning, so we wind up with <u>son</u>. Then, we add another letter to the end of <u>son</u> to get <u>song.</u> When we move to the bottom row, we know that as we move from left to right, we will start with a base word. From the base word, we add a letter at the beginning to get the second word, and we add an additional letter to the end to get the third word. The word that would complete this scenario is <u>man</u>. Students might be tempted to choose answer B, <u>san</u>; however, we know that the answer option has to correspond with the third word in the row.

13. Correct Answer: E

In this series, each drawing is made up of an inner and an outer shape. Each inner shape has an arrow attached, and the arrow rotates counterclockwise 90 degrees between each shape as we move from left to right. Therefore, we expect that the missing shape will be one with an arrow attached at the bottom of its inner shape. We can eliminate choices A and D because the arrow in these shapes is not at the bottom. In choice C the arrow is attached at the bottom of the outer shape rather than at the bottom of the inner shape. To make our final selection between choices B and E, we observe that the outer shapes of the given four drawings in this series are all different from each other: circle, square, hexagon and triangle. The hexagon outer shape in choice B has already been used as an outer shape in the third drawing of the series. Therefore, the missing drawing must be one with a new different outer shape, which is the diamond in choice E.

14. Correct Answer: A

The key with this question is making sure that both words make sense in the given context. Any of the first words in the answer options would make sense: we can 'wash', 'clean', 'find', 'dirty' or 'wipe' dishes. However, the second answer option must make sense together with the first word. Only the words in choice A work together in the blanks to make a complete thought.

15. Correct Answer: C

In the first pair of this figural analogy, each of the two drawings is comprised of an outer shape and inner shape. The outer shape changes from a circle to a triangle and the inner shape stays the same, but changes from light to dark. Similar traits must be applied to the second pair, which has an outer shape that is a square and an inner shape that is a light circle. The outer shape must change from a square, which eliminates choice B. Choices A and D are eliminated because the circles inside do not change from light to dark. Choice E is eliminated because the inner shape is a square and not a circle. Only choice C has an outer shape that is different than a square and a circle that has changed from light to dark.

16. Correct Answer: B

In figuring out this questions, students need to put the words of the analogy into a sentence. This helps with determining the relationship. We could say, "Grass is a small part of a plain." The only answer that also fulfills this relationship is option B, as we could say "sand is

Answers Explanations Practice Test 2

a small part of the beach." Students may be tempted to choose <u>water is to ocean</u>; however, this question goes beyond a simple part to whole relationship. The key is that the first item in the analogy is a very small, individual component of a much larger whole.

17. Correct Answer: A

The pattern in the first two boxes shows that the first number is multiplied by 2 to give the second number, and then the second number is multiplied by 4 to give the third number. In the first box 1x2=2 and 2x4=8. In the second box 2x2=4 and 4x4=16. Therefore, in the third box, 3x2=6 and 6x4=24, so the correct answer is A.

18. Correct Answer: B

The correct answer to this question is choice B because you cannot eat a meal unless you have food to eat. The other answer options might be a part of the meal-eating experience, but they are not vital to what makes a meal.

19. Correct Answer: B

Students can find this sentence by first grouping the words "Sarah found" and "the toy's batteries." Students can then figure out that the best place for the word "never" would be between "Sarah" and "found." The sentence, once arranged, should therefore be "Sarah never found the toy's batteries." Therefore, "never" is the second word, so the answer is option B as "n" is the first letter of the second word.

20. Correct Answer: E

In the top row, we can see that between the first two circles: a) the diagonal line changes direction (from upper-left to lower-right in the first circle, to lower-left to upper-right in the second circle) b) the small star changes position (from the top of the first circle to the bottom of the second circle) and c) the highlighting of the small star alternates (from light in the first circle to dark in the second circle). The third circle has all the traits of the previous two designs combined: two diagonal lines and two small stars. The highlighting again alternates from dark in the previous design to light. This pattern must be applied in the second row to find the second square. First of all, we eliminate choice C as it is a circle and not a square. We also eliminate choices A and B because the direction of the diagonal line does not change from the first design. Since the first square has a small dark arrow on the bottom, we need to find a square with a light arrow on top. Choices D and E both have a small arrow on top, but only in choice E does the arrow change to light. So, E is the correct answer.

21. Correct Answer: C

The pattern in the first two boxes shows that the second number is calculated by multiplying the first number by 4. In the first box 2x4=8. In the second box 3x4=12. You could also say that we can divide the second number by 4 to get the first number. In the first box 8/4=2. In the second box 12/4=3. Therefore, to get the missing number in the third box we can divide 20 by 4. Since 20/4=5, the correct answer is C.

Origins Publications ©

22. Correct Answer: D

This series is made up of alternating letters and two-digit numbers. The last number before the question mark is 17, which means that the missing term that follows must be a letter. Choices B and E can be eliminated since they are numbers. Focusing on just the letters, we can see that they progress by skipping every other letter starting from A as shown in the following pattern:

A B̸ C D̸ E F̸ G H̸ I....

Since we will skip the letter that comes after G, the next letter must be I. The correct answer is D.

23. Correct Answer: B

The pattern in the first two boxes shows that if we add 3 to the first number we get the second number, and if we add 3 to the second number we get the third number. In the first box 9+3=12 and 12+3=15. In the second box 7+3=10 and 10+3=13. Therefore, if we subtract 3 from the third number of the third box we will find the number that is missing: 11-3=8. To test the pattern in the third box we can use 5+3=8 and 8+3=11. The missing number is 8, which means the correct answer is B.

24. Correct Answer: C

In order to answer this question, students must recognize that each of the words in the first row starts with "ca." If we apply this same rule to the second row, we know that each word must start with "sh." The only answer choice that works for this rule is option C.

25. Correct Answer: D

This question asks students for the antonym of <u>clean</u>. Students might be drawn to the answer '<u>spotless</u>'; however, this is a synonym rather than an antonym of <u>clean</u>. Additionally, though something <u>rusted</u> or <u>old</u> might not be <u>clean</u>, these answer choices aren't exactly the opposite of clean. The only true opposite in this question is answer choice D.

26. Correct Answer: E

With this question, students must differentiate what *could* be true from what we know for certain is true. Based on the information provided, we know with certainty that Spencer has at least nine prizes because he has more prizes than Todd, who has eight total. The other answer options are assumptions that *could* be true but which aren't necessarily.

27. Correct Answer: E

In order to answer this question, students need to tackle this problem step by step. First of all, we know that Stacy has a total of 34 papers. Of those, she has 10 red papers. Therefore, 24 of the papers must be either green or blue. We also know that she has 3 times as many green papers as blue papers. In order to figure out how many she has of each, students need to figure out that they are dealing with a 3:1 ratio. We're essentially dividing 24 into four parts (3 parts green, 1 part blue). We know that 24 divided by those 4 parts is 6. So, if Stacy has 3 parts green, we can multiply 3 x 6 to get 18. Therefore, option E is the correct answer.

28.   Correct Answer: E

There is no obvious algebraic relationship among the numbers of each row. Taking a look at the columns, we notice that in the second column the numbers are 14, 21, 28, which are all multiples of 7. Each of the numbers in the first column is one more than the number that was multiplied by 7 in the second column. For example, 2x7 = 14 and the number next to 14 on the left is 3 which is 1 more than 2. Similarly, 3x7=21 and the number on its left is 4 which is one more than 3. Therefore, we understand that if we subtract 1 from the first number and then multiply the difference by 7, we will get the second number. ((3-1) x7=14, (4-1)x7=21, (5-1)x7=28). Now that we have identified the rule between the first and second number in each row, we can determine whether a similar rule applies between the second and the third number, or maybe between the first and the third numbers. Looking at the third column we can see that if we subtract one from the first number and multiply the difference by 9, we will get the third number ((3-1)x9=18 and (5-1)x9=36). So, if we apply this rule in the second row we will find the missing number: (4-1)x9=3x9=27. Therefore, the correct answer is E.

29.   Correct Answer: C

In figuring out the answer to this question, students have to arrange the words into a sentence first. The key is figuring out which word would make the best subject of the sentence. We is the only word that would work well as a subject. Once students have figured out this first word, they then have to ask themselves which word could possibly follow this subject, and they may recognize that it should be a verb. Therefore, the only option in terms of a second word is met. From there, students should be able to complete the sentence. It should read, "We met in science class." Since the third word is in, we know that answer choice C is correct.

30.   Correct Answer: D

To figure out this sentence, students have to use context clues. The clue here is she usually dressed plainly. This should signal to us that, to fill in the blank, we need a word that is the opposite of plain. The best answer, then, is fancy. Students might be tempted to fill in the blank with unique or feminine; however, we once again have to go back to the key context clue. Neither of these words are really the opposite of plain.

31.   Correct Answer: C

In order to answer this question, we have to try and categorize the given answer choices. Each answer is a different type of tree, except for option C. Acorns come from trees but they aren't a type of tree themselves.

32.   Correct Answer: C

If we make pairs of numbers in this series, we will get four pairs (29 and 13,   27 and 13,   ? and 13, and 23 and 13). The second number in each pair is always 13, and the first number in each pair is decreasing by 2 starting from 29. Since the missing number is the first number of the third pair, it must be 29-2-2=25. Therefore, the correct answer is C.

33.   Correct Answer: C

In this pattern matrix, we see a series of circles with a diagonal line through them with shaded arrows inside. The arrows are curved when they point to the left or right and straight when pointing up or down. Also, in each row, the arrow changes its pointing direction counterclockwise by 90 degrees. For example, in the first row it starts pointing to the right, then upwards and then to the left. Since the drawing in the third row before the question mark has its arrow pointing down, we know we are looking for a drawing with an arrow pointing to the right. Therefore, we can eliminate choice D which has an arrow pointing to the left. We can also eliminate choice E because although the arrow is pointing to the right, it is not curved as it should be. Additionally, we can eliminate choice B because the arrow is drawn above the diagonal line of the circle instead of being behind it as in all drawings in the matrix. In order to choose among the remaining choices of A and C, students need to pay attention to the direction of the diagonal lines in the matrix. We see that when the arrow is pointing to the right, the diagonal has an upper-left to bottom-right direction. When the arrow is pointing to the left, the diagonal has an upper-right to bottom-left direction. Since we are also looking for a right pointing arrow, the direction of the diagonal must have an upper-left to bottom-right direction. Thus, the correct answer is C.

34.   Correct Answer: D

In this number matrix, we need to identify the relationship between the two pairs of numbers and the series of four numbers. In the first row, we can see that the four number series is created by switching the numbers in the first pair to get the first and third number in the series of four numbers. The second and the fourth number in the series of four numbers are the second pair of numbers in their original order. The same pattern must be applied to the second row. The second and the fourth numbers in the four number series are 4 and 9, which is the pair of numbers we are looking for. Therefore, the correct answer is D.

35.   Correct Answer: D

In the first pair of this figural analogy, we can see that the shape of the two combined triangles remains the same and the small circle inside stays in the same position but alternates from light to dark. A similar pattern must be applied to the second pair. The overall shape, which is a square with a vertical line, must remain the same. Choices B and E are eliminated as they are squares with horizontal lines. The triangle must be in the same position on the right but change from dark to light. Therefore, choice D is the correct answer.

36.   Correct Answer: C

To answer this question, we must first figure out that 3x7=21. Then, we know that 21-5=16.

37.   Correct Answer: D

As with all analogies, it is helpful to put the words into a sentence to discern their relationship. We could say, "coffee is a type of beverage." Our next step would be to say, "pie is a type of_____." Based on this, the only answer that works is dessert.

38.   Correct Answer: B

In this series of numbers and letters each letter is followed by a pair of numbers. The letter E is followed by the pair 7 2, the letter G is followed by the pair 12 5, etc. Since we are looking for what follows the letter K, we understand that this should be the first number of the pair of numbers. Choice A can be eliminated as it is a letter rather than a number. In order to find what number goes where the question mark is, we need to reveal the relationship between the numbers and the letters. Exploring the triple E 7 2, we observe that the difference between the numbers is 7-2=5, and E is the 5th letter of the alphabet. Moving to the triple G 12 5, we also see that the difference is 12-5=7 and G is the 7th letter of the alphabet. The pattern continues for the group I 19 10, where 19-10=9 and I is the 9th letter of the alphabet . Therefore, since K is the 11th letter of the alphabet, the number that follows it must be 11 greater than 16. Therefore, the missing number is 27 since 27-16=11 and K is the 11th letter of the alphabet. The correct answer is B.

39.   Correct Answer: E

The pattern in the first row of the box shows that we are adding 13 as we move from left to right (5+13=18 and 18+13=31). The same rule applies on the first two numbers in the second row (11+13=24). Therefore, since 13+24=37, the correct answer is E.

40.   Correct Answer: A

To figure out the answer to this question, students have to discover the pattern of the words in the box. Looking at the top row, we have the word <u>eat</u> in the first column. This serves as a base word in the pattern. The next word adds and a "b" to the beginning to get "beat." The third word adds an "s" to the base word to get "seat." We know then that, in the second row, we must follow the same pattern. So if <u>ate</u> is the base word, we need to add a "b" in the second column to get "bate." Since the third column also adds an "s" to the base word to get <u>sate</u>, we know the second row is adding the same letters to the base word as the first row. Option D may be a tempting answer, but it is not correct because the added letter must be a "b."

41.   Correct Answer: B

Each drawing in this pattern matrix is comprised of a hexagon with two diagonals and a small circle. In each row, as we progress from left to right, the small circle moves in a downward vertical direction. In the first row, it starts from outside of the hexagon, then moves down to the top of the hexagon, and then moves down again so that it is inside the upper triangle of the hexagon. In the second row, the small circle again moves downward from the top of the hexagon so that it is inside the upper triangle of the hexagon, and then moves down again so that it is at the center of the hexagon. At the same time, the circle alternates between light and dark as we go through the drawings in each row. The circle in the drawing in the third row before the question mark is located at the center of the hexagon. If it moves down, it will be inside the lower triangle of the hexagon. We also know that the next figure will have a light circle. We can eliminate choices C and D as they have dark circles. We can also eliminate choice E because the circle moved down too far, and choice A because the circle did not move. The only drawing with a light circle inside the hexagon at the bottom is B. Therefore, the correct answer is B.

42. Correct Answer: C

This question requires students to choose only the answer choice that provides information about something we know for certain. Based on the information provided in the question, we know that Mrs. Smith assigned homework on four days—Monday, Tuesday, Wednesday, and Friday. We also know that Mr. Carter assigned homework a maximum of three days, but we don't know which days for sure. We know that Ms. Davis may have assigned as many as two days of homework, but we don't know how many exactly or if she assigned homework at all. The only answer option was can say is true for certain is choice C.

43. Correct Answer: E

The pattern, moving from left to right, is to alternate addition of 11 and subtraction of 4 as shown below:

7 (+11) 18 (-4) 14 (+11) 25 (-4) 21 (+11) 32

Since 32-4=28, we can identify the correct answer as E.

44. Correct Answer: C

The first pair of this figural analogy has three circles inside the triangle for the first drawing and then three circles aligned horizontally in the second drawing. In the second drawing two of the circles have been move outside the triangle. Since the same pattern must be applied to the second pair of drawings, we need to find a drawing of a circle with three triangles aligned horizontally that has two of the triangles outside the circle and one triangle inside the circle. Choice D is eliminated because there are circles outside the circle rather than triangles. Choice E is eliminated because the triangle inside the circle has been rotated by 180 degrees. Choice A is eliminated because the triangles outside the circle are not the same as the one inside. Choice B is eliminated because the two triangles are partially inside the circle instead of being totally outside. Therefore, the correct answer is C.

45. Correct Answer: B

In figuring out the opposite of the word "hot", students have to keep in mind the difference between something that is hot versus merely warm. Hot is more of an extreme, so the answer is <u>cold</u> rather than <u>cool</u>. Though <u>snow</u> is cold, it isn't an exact opposite of hot. <u>Fire</u> and <u>warm</u> are related to the word <u>hot</u>, however, neither is the opposite of "hot".

46. Correct Answer: C

Students must figure out that this question is dealing with a total of five parts: 4 parts fiction books and 1 part nonfiction books. If we divide 60 books by 5 parts, we get 12. So, if Madison has 4 times as many fiction books as nonfiction books, we know she has 12 nonfiction books and 48 fiction books.

47. Correct Answer: A

To answer this question, we first have to arrange the sentence. The best completed sentence in this question would read, "The party will be at Timothy's house." Based on this completed sentence, the first word is <u>the</u>. Therefore, since this starts with a "t," the correct answer is A.

48. Correct Answer: E

Each figure in the first row of this pattern matrix is comprised of a specific number of thin bars that are crossed by a diagonal with a direction from bottom-left to upper-right. As we move from left to right the bars increase by one, alternate between light and dark, and alternate their direction between horizontal and vertical. Since the second drawing of the second row has four light vertical bars, students need to look for a shape with five dark horizontal bars. Choice A can be eliminated because it has four bars. Choice C and D can be eliminated because they have light bars. Choice B can also be eliminated because, although it has five highlighted and horizontal bars, the diagonal line that crosses the bars goes from up-left to bottom-right instead of up-right to bottom-left as is the case in all drawings. Therefore, the correct answer is E.

49. Correct Answer: D

In order to read a book, you must read <u>words</u>. While a teacher, pictures, story, or other people might be part of the reading experience, they are not required to read a book.

50. Correct Answer: E

In this series, each drawing is comprised of an outer shape that is filled with a group of identical smaller shapes. The outer shape alternates between a square and a hexagon. The number of the smaller inner shapes decreases by 1 as we move from left to right. The inner shapes also alternate between dark and light. The inner shape is never repeated between designs. Since the outer shape in the fourth drawing is a hexagon, we expect that the outer shape of the next drawing will be a square, so choice A is eliminated. As there are two stars inside the fourth drawing of the series we know that the missing drawing will have only one shape inside, so choice D can be eliminated. As the two stars inside the fourth drawing are light, we know that the drawing we are looking for will have one dark inner shape so choice C can be eliminated. Finally, choice B can also be eliminated, because the dark shape inside the square is a diamond, which was already used in the third drawing. Therefore, the correct answer is E

51. Correct Answer: A

The pattern in the first row of the box shows that we are adding 3 as we move from left to right (9+3=12 and 12+3=15). The same rule applies on the first two numbers in the second row as 11+3=14. Therefore, since 14+3=17, the correct answer is A.

52. Correct Answer: B

The main shape in this series is a pentagon that alternates between light and dark. Moving from left to right, one small circle is added to a vertex outside the pentagon starting at the top and moving in a clockwise direction. The small circles also alternate between light to dark as they are added, and their shading is reversed between drawings. The fifth drawing must have a dark pentagon, which eliminates choice C. An additional small circle at the lower-left vertex of the pentagon should be included in the fifth design, which eliminates choice E. The existing circles should be shaded the opposite of the fourth drawing, which eliminates choices A and D Therefore, the correct answer is B.

53.   Correct Answer: B

Since Lori fired employees, we can assume she didn't have enough people to work on the project. We can assume, then, that she might <u>postpone</u>, or put off, working on the project until she hires more people.

54.   Correct Answer: D

The first figure of the given pair in this figural analogy is a square which includes a triangle. The square has also a horizontal line which connects two opposite sides. Now, in the second figure of the given pair, the triangle becomes the outer shape with an inside square that has a horizontal line. The same pattern must be applied to the second pair too, which, in the first figure, has a triangle with a square and a vertical line. Students need to notice that the vertical line is a line of the triangle as it connects one of its vertices with the opposite side. Therefore, the figure that we are looking for must be a square which includes a triangle with a vertical line in it. Choices A and C can be eliminated as the outer shapes are triangles and not squares. Choice E can be eliminated because, although it is a square which includes a triangle, the vertical line is not a line of the triangle but of the square. Choice B can also be eliminated because, again, although we have a square which includes a triangle, the vertical line that is drawn is not a line of the triangle as it starts from the triangle's vertex but ends at the side of the square. Therefore, the correct choice is D.

55.   Correct Answer: C

As with other inference questions, the key here is finding the answer that we know is true without any qualifications. We know that Larry has 12 apps; some are games, some educational, and some are for the news. Only 3 apps are games, so we know that there are 9 apps left. Of those 9 apps, some are educational and some are for the news. Since 9 cannot be divided evenly by the two types of apps, we know for certain there is not an even number of educational and news apps.

56.   Correct Answer: B

The rule is that in each box, the first number is multiplied by 7 to get the second number (2x7=14 and 3x7=21). Multiplying the first number of the third box, by 7 we get 4x7=28. The correct answer is B.

57.   Correct Answer: D

To answer this question, we have to find the pattern in the first row. Each of these words starts with the same letter—"s"— and ends with the same letter—"g." Additionally, each word has one more letter than the word before; the first word has three letters, the second has four letters, and the final word has five letters. We know that the second row must follow the same pattern. We know that it must start with a "b," end with a "t" and be five letters in length. The only word that fulfills all of these criteria is "blurt."

58.   Correct Answer: B

The key here is the word <u>played.</u> A piano can only be played using <u>fingers</u>. Though a piano is often played with music sheets or in a musical composition suggestive of a song, someone could very well play the keys of a piano without forming a song.

59. Correct Answer: E

In this pattern matrix, we have two missing numbers in two different rows. In the first row we can see that if we multiply the first number by 6 we get the second number (3x6=18), and if we divide the second number by 2 we get the third number (18/2=9). To determine if this is the pattern for the other rows, we move on by checking the rule partially. Dividing the last two numbers of the second row (36/2=18) shows that the second part of the rule is valid. Multiplying the first number of the third row by 6, we get the second number (7x6=42). Therefore, the pattern that we identified in the first row is also valid for the other two rows. In order to find the first number of the second row, we will divide the second number by 6 (36/6=6). In order to find the third number of the third row, we will divide the second number by 2 (42/2=21). Therefore, the correct answer is E.

60. Correct Answer: D

In the first drawing on the left of this figural analogy, we have a hexagon as the outermost shape, a triangle as the middle shape, and a circle as the innermost shape. This drawing is paired with the drawing where the innermost circle has moved outside the shape, and the remaining two shapes (the hexagon and the triangle) have switched their positions. In addition, all three shapes reversed their shading. In the second pair the innermost square must move outside the shape and change from dark to light. Choice B is eliminated because the square is light and choice E is eliminated because a circle was moved outside the shape. Now, the diamond and the circle must switch places and reverse their shading. Choice A is eliminated because the circle and the diamond are both dark. Choice C is eliminated because the there is a pentagon inside the circle instead of a diamond. Therefore, choice D is the correct answer.

61. Correct Answer: E

In this series, the number of shaded diamonds increases by 2 as we progress form left to right. The shaded diamonds also alternate their direction from vertical to horizontal. Additionally, when aligned vertically, the shaded diamonds are on the left side of the grid and when aligned horizontally they are on the top part of the grid. Since the fourth drawing has 8 shaded diamonds aligned horizontally, we expect that the missing drawing will have 10 shaded diamonds aligned vertically. Choice B is eliminated because the 10 shaded diamonds are aligned horizontally. Neither choice A or C has 10 shaded diamonds, so they are eliminated. Choices D and E both have 10 shaded diamonds aligned vertically, but in choice D, the shading is along the right side of the grid, so choice D is eliminated. Choice E is the correct answer.

62. Correct Answer: E

While each of these words has to do with math, fractions are not a process in the same way that addition, subtraction, multiplication, and division are.

63. Correct Answer: A

In order to answer this question, we must figure out that 6 x 8 = 48. Then, 48 + 4 = 52.

64. Correct Answer: E

In this series, each drawing is either an outer circle containing a smaller circle with an arrow attached, or an outer square containing a smaller square with an arrow attached. The drawings alternate between circles and squares. Since the fourth drawing is a square we expect that the missing drawing will be a circle, so choice C is eliminated. Choice B is also eliminated because it is a circle with a square inside instead of a circle. The arrows between the two circles drawings rotate counterclockwise 90 degrees, so the next position should be at the bottom-right side of the circle. Choice A and D are eliminated because the arrows did not rotate 90 degrees. The correct answer is E.

65. Correct Answer: E

This question requires students to figure out the nuances among these words. <u>Jump</u>, <u>pounce</u>, <u>leap</u>, and <u>spring</u> are all synonyms. However, the word <u>skip</u> is slightly different because it has to do with bouncing back and forth from one foot to another. So, while it is similar, it is not an exact synonym for the other words.

66. Correct Answer: A

In the first row of this matrix, as we move from left to right, students need to notice that initially there is a diagonal in the square from the lower-left to the upper-right. Then a diagonal from the upper-left to the lower-right is added. Finally, the bottom-right part of this diagonal is cut and placed next to the top side of the square. This pattern must be applied to the second row too, where we have a triangle which initially has a right to left diagonal segment inside and then it also gets a left to right diagonal segment which intersects with the first one. Therefore, the third drawing must be a triangle with the bottom right piece of the diagonal segment transferred next to the top side of the triangle. Choice D is eliminated because it is a square. Choice B is eliminated because no piece of either diagonal segment has been cut. Choice C is eliminated because both the bottom parts of the two diagonal segments have been removed. Choice E is eliminated because the bottom left piece of a diagonal segment has been cut and transferred instead of the bottom right segment of the other diagonal. Therefore, the correct answer is A.

67. Correct Answer: D

If we add 4 to the first number of the first box we will get the second number (2+4=6). In the second box, if we add 5 to the first number we will get the second number (4+5=9). Therefore, the pattern in the first two boxes shows that the number that is added to the first number of each box increases by 1 as we move from left to right. So, in order to find the second number in the third box, we need to add 6 to the first number. Since 6+6=12, the correct answer is D.

68. Correct Answer: C

If <u>enter</u> means to "go in," then we need a word that means to "go out." Therefore, <u>exit</u> is the best answer choice. Students might be distracted by <u>in</u>, <u>entrance</u>, or <u>go</u> but these are not the correct answers because they are closer to synonyms than antonyms. Additionally, <u>finish</u> is not correct as it has no real correlation to enter.

69.   Correct Answer: A

The pattern in the first two boxes shows that the second number is obtained by dividing the first number by 4 (12/4=3 and 20/4=5). Therefore, if we divide 32 by 4 we will get the missing number. Since 32/4=8, the correct answer is A.

70.   Correct Answer: C

The pattern in the first row of the box shows that we are subtracting 5 as we move from left to right (23-5=18 and 18-5=13). The same rule applies on the first two numbers in the second row (19-5=14). Since 14-5=9, the correct answer is C.

71.   Correct Answer: B

In the first drawing on the left of this figural analogy, we have an unshaded hexagon with a shaded triangle inside. This drawing is paired with a drawing where the triangle has moved to the top outside of the hexagon and both shapes have reversed their shading. The same pattern must be applied to the second pair, which means that we are looking for a shaded triangle with an unshaded diamond above its vertex on top. Choices C and E are eliminated because the base figure is not a triangle. Choice A is eliminated because the triangle is not shaded. Choice D is eliminated because the shape above the triangle's vertex at the top is a pentagon and not a diamond. Therefore, the correct answer is B.

72.   Correct Answer: E

The pattern in this matrix is that we divide each number by 4 to find the next one in the same row (32/4=8 and 8/4=2 for the first row and 48/4=12 for the second row). To find the missing number we divide 12 by 4, which equals 3. The correct answer is E.

Origins Publications ©

Origins Publications

Use a No. 2 Pencil.
Fill-in Bubble Completely.
Ⓐ Ⓑ Ⓒ ● Ⓔ

Name: _____   Date: _____

1. Ⓐ Ⓑ Ⓒ Ⓓ Ⓔ   19. Ⓐ Ⓑ Ⓒ Ⓓ Ⓔ   37. Ⓐ Ⓑ Ⓒ Ⓓ Ⓔ   55. Ⓐ Ⓑ Ⓒ Ⓓ Ⓔ

2. Ⓐ Ⓑ Ⓒ Ⓓ Ⓔ   20. Ⓐ Ⓑ Ⓒ Ⓓ Ⓔ   38. Ⓐ Ⓑ Ⓒ Ⓓ Ⓔ   56. Ⓐ Ⓑ Ⓒ Ⓓ Ⓔ

3. Ⓐ Ⓑ Ⓒ Ⓓ Ⓔ   21. Ⓐ Ⓑ Ⓒ Ⓓ Ⓔ   39. Ⓐ Ⓑ Ⓒ Ⓓ Ⓔ   57. Ⓐ Ⓑ Ⓒ Ⓓ Ⓔ

4. Ⓐ Ⓑ Ⓒ Ⓓ Ⓔ   22. Ⓐ Ⓑ Ⓒ Ⓓ Ⓔ   40. Ⓐ Ⓑ Ⓒ Ⓓ Ⓔ   58. Ⓐ Ⓑ Ⓒ Ⓓ Ⓔ

5. Ⓐ Ⓑ Ⓒ Ⓓ Ⓔ   23. Ⓐ Ⓑ Ⓒ Ⓓ Ⓔ   41. Ⓐ Ⓑ Ⓒ Ⓓ Ⓔ   59. Ⓐ Ⓑ Ⓒ Ⓓ Ⓔ

6. Ⓐ Ⓑ Ⓒ Ⓓ Ⓔ   24. Ⓐ Ⓑ Ⓒ Ⓓ Ⓔ   42. Ⓐ Ⓑ Ⓒ Ⓓ Ⓔ   60. Ⓐ Ⓑ Ⓒ Ⓓ Ⓔ

7. Ⓐ Ⓑ Ⓒ Ⓓ Ⓔ   25. Ⓐ Ⓑ Ⓒ Ⓓ Ⓔ   43. Ⓐ Ⓑ Ⓒ Ⓓ Ⓔ   61. Ⓐ Ⓑ Ⓒ Ⓓ Ⓔ

8. Ⓐ Ⓑ Ⓒ Ⓓ Ⓔ   26. Ⓐ Ⓑ Ⓒ Ⓓ Ⓔ   44. Ⓐ Ⓑ Ⓒ Ⓓ Ⓔ   62. Ⓐ Ⓑ Ⓒ Ⓓ Ⓔ

9. Ⓐ Ⓑ Ⓒ Ⓓ Ⓔ   27. Ⓐ Ⓑ Ⓒ Ⓓ Ⓔ   45. Ⓐ Ⓑ Ⓒ Ⓓ Ⓔ   63. Ⓐ Ⓑ Ⓒ Ⓓ Ⓔ

10. Ⓐ Ⓑ Ⓒ Ⓓ Ⓔ   28. Ⓐ Ⓑ Ⓒ Ⓓ Ⓔ   46. Ⓐ Ⓑ Ⓒ Ⓓ Ⓔ   64. Ⓐ Ⓑ Ⓒ Ⓓ Ⓔ

11. Ⓐ Ⓑ Ⓒ Ⓓ Ⓔ   29. Ⓐ Ⓑ Ⓒ Ⓓ Ⓔ   47. Ⓐ Ⓑ Ⓒ Ⓓ Ⓔ   65. Ⓐ Ⓑ Ⓒ Ⓓ Ⓔ

12. Ⓐ Ⓑ Ⓒ Ⓓ Ⓔ   30. Ⓐ Ⓑ Ⓒ Ⓓ Ⓔ   48. Ⓐ Ⓑ Ⓒ Ⓓ Ⓔ   66. Ⓐ Ⓑ Ⓒ Ⓓ Ⓔ

13. Ⓐ Ⓑ Ⓒ Ⓓ Ⓔ   31. Ⓐ Ⓑ Ⓒ Ⓓ Ⓔ   49. Ⓐ Ⓑ Ⓒ Ⓓ Ⓔ   67. Ⓐ Ⓑ Ⓒ Ⓓ Ⓔ

14. Ⓐ Ⓑ Ⓒ Ⓓ Ⓔ   32. Ⓐ Ⓑ Ⓒ Ⓓ Ⓔ   50. Ⓐ Ⓑ Ⓒ Ⓓ Ⓔ   68. Ⓐ Ⓑ Ⓒ Ⓓ Ⓔ

15. Ⓐ Ⓑ Ⓒ Ⓓ Ⓔ   33. Ⓐ Ⓑ Ⓒ Ⓓ Ⓔ   51. Ⓐ Ⓑ Ⓒ Ⓓ Ⓔ   69. Ⓐ Ⓑ Ⓒ Ⓓ Ⓔ

16. Ⓐ Ⓑ Ⓒ Ⓓ Ⓔ   34. Ⓐ Ⓑ Ⓒ Ⓓ Ⓔ   52. Ⓐ Ⓑ Ⓒ Ⓓ Ⓔ   70. Ⓐ Ⓑ Ⓒ Ⓓ Ⓔ

17. Ⓐ Ⓑ Ⓒ Ⓓ Ⓔ   35. Ⓐ Ⓑ Ⓒ Ⓓ Ⓔ   53. Ⓐ Ⓑ Ⓒ Ⓓ Ⓔ   71. Ⓐ Ⓑ Ⓒ Ⓓ Ⓔ

18. Ⓐ Ⓑ Ⓒ Ⓓ Ⓔ   36. Ⓐ Ⓑ Ⓒ Ⓓ Ⓔ   54. Ⓐ Ⓑ Ⓒ Ⓓ Ⓔ   72. Ⓐ Ⓑ Ⓒ Ⓓ Ⓔ

Made in the USA
Las Vegas, NV
29 October 2022

58420876R00024